Amber
Returns to Maine!

And Other
Songs of the Soul

By:

Susan C. Haley

ISBN 0-7414-5859-4

Printed in the United States of America

Published March 2010

INFINITY PUBLISHING
1094 New DeHaven Street, Suite 100
West Conshohocken, PA 19428-2713
Toll-free (877) BUY BOOK
Local Phone (610) 941-9999
Fax (610) 941-9959
Info@buybooksontheweb.com
www.buybooksontheweb.com

Dedicated
To the memory of
Jerry A. Haley
1943 – 1999

~

And Our Sons
Bill and Vincent

"I went to the woods because I wished to live deliberately, to front only the essential facts of life, and see if I could not learn what it had to teach, and not, when I came to die, discover that I had not lived."

~ Henry David Thoreau ~

Acknowledgments

To my lifetime on this Earth and all the experiences and inspirations that molded me into what I am. The grandmother, the parents, the sister, the relatives, and my own family, husband and two sons, who helped forge my pathways, wherever they led.

To the teachers and the classic writers who broadened my mind to realize the power of the written word. To those like Thoreau and Emerson, Bach and Whitman, who taught me the value of rejecting society's standards and fraudulent values while embracing the wise and the natural.

To the relatives and friends, dear, present and past, even those unknown, who've shared a gene, made a mark, and wrote a lyric in my songs.

And to the animals, both wild and domestic, that have so touched my life and my Spirit. They are all a part of me, this Earth and all its creatures.

Susan Haley ~ 2010

Contents

The Inner Nuances of the Soul

We all have at least one alter-ego, that person hidden inside who we either wish we could be or who, over a lifetime, is a genuine part of us.

I have an obsession for nuances whether hidden in a word, a thought, or in a tenet of spirituality. I believe in the triune nature of most everything. Every utterance, written or spoken, prompts a different perspective in the mind of the reader or listener. Our understanding of those words initiates from the preponderance of prior perceptions, emotions and experiences we've had. We are creatures of our perceptions. There are many 'truths' in the collective mind. The ultimate *Truth*, I suspect, is unknown in this dimension.

For me, pulling from this non-ending source of inner rumblings is what gives the writer in me the courage to fly free above the rules and admonitions of genre and grammatical language. For a writer, metaphor evolves into the absolute. Fantasy can become fact, and dreams can become attainable goals. This is especially so if the words and the personalities are pulled from your very soul.

Simple lines of strung-together words began tumbling out of me on lined yellow paper as soon as I was able to draw clumsy, rather lopsided letters, probably the age of four or so. For nigh over sixty years now, I've been dribbling my soul onto a page. Its *voice* gave birth to Amber and Sucarha, and the words of my poems and stories. I don't create them driven by a muse like most good writers do.

The objective part of my mind steps back and the subjective inner voices begin to sing of joy, love, gaiety, even silly fun. Perhaps they shout in rage! Perhaps the tone is of fear, confusion, hurt, or pain. The ebony of darkness or despair may linger in the shadows between the lines.

For me, no other writing genre affords more complete expression than poetry or impassioned poetical prose. Whether in a few but powerful words, a saga, a column, an article or for-my-eyes-only ramblings, it's one of my three personalities talking.

Philosophies, principles, perceptions, and experiences emerge in verse. Memories stored for decades, or hopes for that yet coming, sing out with the crescendo of a symphony, the passion of a compelling solo, or simply . . . humming silence.

Before I can take you back to Maine with Amber, I must share how Amber came to go there.

The Essence of a Poet

A heart sense nestled in a wisp of humanity,
A mind sense of letters and sounds
dribbled on a page.
Words reaching far beyond vanity,
More, the Cosmic emanations of a sage.

Not words draped over casual feelings,
or descriptive tenets
labored by a passing muse,
but passions, emotions, facades peeling,
stripping away all of conditioning's ruse.

They bare a soul sense, a gut sense,
their very being,
a sharing of innermost value and wealth.
Thoughtful ponderings that see,
deep into the chasms and valleys of 'self'.

Verbal energies, of love and of Earth,
utterings wrenched from an inner store,
shout quietly, of the Divinity
inherent in their very core.

In poems of the sensual, the playful child,
in antics or drama, or lyrics of life,
their truths are revealed
through their songs and their strife.

To those fortunate
to have read them, or heard,
they forge a path, then share their light.
Regardless, the era, the age, of their words,
memory's halls hold them forever in sight.

So utter on, dear poets,
your dabblings of pen,
your heartcries and fears.
Speak ever on, dear poets,
To all those Who'll listen and hear . . .

Uncertainty

I begin this book with the era which likely impacted the path of the person I was to become. The forces prior had molded my parents and their parents before them, and the circumstances and effects of those generations would sculpt my inner being. That is the circular way of things in this life. What goes around does come back around. Perhaps, with a different result.

World War II was the great separator of fathers and their children. Often dads came home to meet, in the flesh, three or four year old children for the very first time. Still in their mother's womb, or only days or weeks old when their dad left, children were thrust into the arms of what were to them, total strangers. Did they really understand when told their dad was far, far away fighting a war to keep them safe? Did the occasional photo really embrace the depth of the relationship for the dad? The tribute following depicts that kind of meeting between me and my dad. I was three and a half.

Uncertainty

Uncertainty – hidden under hairbows,
a hat slightly askew.
Behind wide, child eyes,
and glasses tinted blue.

Uncertainty – in rumpled underwear,
and wrinkled sergeant's stripes.
They wear a hint of resistance
When thrust into an unknown existence.

Uncertainty . . .
this being a daughter,
this being a dad.
Strangers, robbed by war,
of sharing what we had.

Hands almost touching,
yet afraid to grab hold.
Uncertain of the outcome,
of trusting what'd been told.

I study, now, the shadows,
the stiff, determined knees,
the high top brown of sturdy shoes,
the desire to run free . . .
Did this uncertainty form the soul of me?

I wonder now, while peering
into the eyes of that daughter,
at the timid hand that dad wore . . .
Did this uncertainty
birth my hate for war?

Did it birth my pondering mind?
Mold a writer or some such?
Instill the insatiable curiosity . . . ?
I'm certain of so little,
driven by so much.

I wonder now,
if that first uncertain meeting,
now robbed again by death,
will once again repeat itself
when I draw my final breath?

Will dad be there
to meet this daughter
when I come upon that shore
As I was here to meet him
when he came home from war?

Susan Haley ~ 2009

Epitaph For a Man

What are the standards
that it's said must be met
for a life to be deemed worthy,
well-lived and well-spent?
What are the marks to be put on the chart
where accomplishments are listed,
where you played your part?

Must you be a general in matters of war?
Make profound discoveries,
change the world evermore?
Or could all your achievements
in the wars of worldly toils
be specially marked by four years
of service on war's foreign soils?

Must you do something profound
that brings kudos and worldwide fame?
Or will fifty years of dedication
and hard work bring you the same?
Must you leave behind great notoriety
and huge stores of wealth?
Or a family loved, secure, and in health?

Need you be a doctor,
a lawyer,
a teacher or some such?
Or a simple man, with a tireless desire,
which truly meant so much?

I knew a man, who had no greater goal
over eight decades of life,
than to provide, care for, and make happy,
two daughters and a wife.
I knew a man who only these basic,
these simple things, did . . .

I called him "Papa",
And for me, no greater name,
has ever been said.

Susan Haley ~ December 13, 2005

    Written for my dad, William Robert Ball, in the evening of the day he left this earth and soared high . . . free, free at last. The preceding poem, *Uncertainty*, was written afterward in a time of my ponderings. Together, they are the Alpha and the Omega of a daughter and a dad. There was a lifetime in between.

Cleelen Williams

Cleelen, a unique, old English name. I've never heard it, or seen it, since the equally unique woman that carried it left this place. To me, it didn't matter; I called her "Gram."

At what age of infancy I was brought to Gram has escaped my memory, but she was the one who nurtured my soul, I think. She was the one who I bonded with at that time of life when forever bonds are made. It remained so until my dad came home from the war and he and my mother bought a small house and took me there, and it remains so until this very day, though Gram soared free many years ago.

During the war years, my mother worked and my grandpa worked. Gram took care of me and the jobs of the kitchen, the laundry, and whatever else time allowed. Mother and her sister, Elnora, who also lived at home and worked, helped with the heavy housework and ironing at the end of a long day. Times were hard back then. War is always hard on families, and my grandparents had already clawed their way through WW1 and The Great

Depression, too. Hard work and struggle were all they knew, and I suppose to them, that was just the way of life in those days and times.

My grandpa, who'd immigrated here from Cornwall, England to work in the coal mines of Pennsylvania, eventually settled in the Upper Peninsula of Michigan. There, he became a copper miner. *The Copper Country* they called it in the Keweenaw Peninsula of the U.P. Years of working a mile under the earth, chopping enough wood for cooking, bathing and warmth and, wife at his side, growing and preserving your own food takes a special kind of work ethic generally unknown in this country today.

It was a long hard depression in the cold country of the U.P. and my grandpa moved his family to Pontiac, Michigan when General Motors and the auto factories revamped to make war machines instead of cars, busses and trucks.

Grandpa was over age to go to the war but he served America and his native England in the Michigan car factories.

I can still see him sitting after supper with his chin cupped in his hands, propped by elbows on knees, listening to the old console radio. There was no television back then. I remember walking to the bus stop to meet him from work when I got a little older. Not many owned cars, either.

But it's Gram that overflows my memories. It was Gram who instilled in me a tender heart, a sense of compassion, a love of the simplest things and a basic domesticity. It was Gram who reinforced the joy of a special, honest and loyal relationship, a nonjudgmental unconditional love, a quiet moment, and how to go it alone when you lose a spouse. It was Gram who inspired me with the heart and mind of a poet without even realizing what a miracle gift she was giving just being what she naturally was.

All through high school, I'd go home to her house after school on Tuesdays. The sun always shone through the kitchen window when we had our breakfast tea on Wednesday morning.

Cleelen's Sunray

A sunray glistens
thru the morning window.
The kettle is boiling
its first cup of tea.

Gentle and kind,
never complaining,
she greets the new day.
And, God is on the sunray.

A simple spirit,
no quest for fortune or fame.
Loving wife, dear mother,
my very best friend,
Gram was her name.

Never a resentment,
angry word or deed,
always there with a smile
when I had a need.
And, God is on the sunray.

Thru the years,
her quiet wisdom grows.
Her acceptance of the solitude,
Of the worth she bestows.

A life led with dignity,
the giving of love,
asking for nothing,
drawing strength from above.
And, God is on the sunray.

The kettle, now, is silent.
The table standing bare.
Family remains, hugging memories close,
telling her they'll always care.

But, the sunray is eternal,
as are the rains . . .
Now, Gram is with God
on the sunray.

Susan Haley ~ 1981 ~

I find it near impossible to comprehend that twenty-eight years have separated us here in this realm. They haven't, really. Death only separates us in flesh. The mind rooms of memory and the Spirit in the heart, the essence there when you need comforting, even the occasional voice in an empty room, are so much more powerful than the death of a body.

If you doubt it, I wish you a sunray when you need one or a walk under the trees on a warm afternoon in a dream.

Doorways

Unknown authors find themselves on a continual search for a podium of sorts in which to display their woven words. Entering contests is an often used venue. I entered one earlier in my writing career sponsored by an organization called *Doorways*. We were to offer a life history in twelve hundred words or less. A life history essay in twelve hundred words or less? How can that be, I asked myself? Quite a feat for one roaming around these life roads for sixty plus years!

I muddled with that until I pondered on the deeper meaning of "Doorways". Life is a series of opening doors, is it not? Each new opening, a small history in itself. Wrestling that thought further, I dressed the *doorway* premise in the triune garb of youth, middle-age, and aged. As in fine wine, of course. Nothing of worth ever gets old, so I'm told. I then decided to use a summation technique to compose my entry.

Passing through the first two doors of my life, and the myriad of rooms behind them, was usual enough. Like everyone, I fell down a lot learning to walk and ride a bike. I learned to share my cookies and milk in Kindergarten, and not to share my gym suit in high school.

On cue, all the right hormones kicked in. I loved and lost the boy next door, experienced the joys of right choices, and learned there were consequences for wrong ones. My soul found its mate and nests were feathered. We had two fine sons to make up our brood and embarked on the building of our lives. Some of our goals were accomplished, others not. Also, typical enough, I suppose.

The door numbered *One* opened unto door number *Two* in ways that are familiar to most. A certain maturity was born and new horizons were sought as the nest emptied and the boys went on to explore and open their own doorways. Now, there were new curiosities needing to be fed, new goals needing to be set. I went back to college later in life deciding to hone the skills of writing which was, and yet remains, my passion. Writing is also my best mode for serious communication, as verbally, I tend to babble or totally clam up.

I did well in school, but still the activities of husband, sons, and home took precedence by my own choice. The writing as a career or simply creating worthy prose of any length remained a dream stored on a back shelf in my mind. Instead, I placated myself with a bit of journalism for local newspapers and tutoring English for the university I attended. Time flowed into the next moment and the circles turned.

It has been said that into each life some rain must fall. Yet, the occasional thunderstorms, we discover, often serve to water our life's gardens. I had my share of vibrant gardens. Gardens that grew hardy with myriads of colorful experiences even among intermittent periods of drought and storm.

But, then, there may just be the infamous *big one*, the hurricane of sorts, brewing in the realms of happenstance, too. Sudden widowhood at age fifty-six slammed my door numbered *Two* quite shut. Suddenly, I found myself standing, minus my right side, at the threshold of a gaping door numbered *Three*. I was unwilling, even unable, to enter the room lying beyond this threshold. In an instant, my gardens were no longer gently watered, but a huge field of mud.

Wallowing, it's often called, when we simply sit and wonder at the 'whys and whats' of circumstance and resolve to feel sorry for ourselves. Oh, I excelled at wallowing. I worked everyday, and put on all the right faces in all the right places. I was lauded for my strength and courage by family and friends, those close to me. It's amazing the wardrobes with which we adorn ourselves over our tattered underwear. My muddy garden had dried, cracked and brittle, into an internal wasteland I was convinced would never bear flowers again.

An avid lover of Nature, I tend to use its many metaphors in conversation. One day while talking with a friend, he noticed a rip in my gaily-colored cape of hiding.

"How are you, really?" he asked.

Taken aback and my mask dislodged, I confessed that the high mountain meadows of my life had disintegrated into a desert of despair and I couldn't seem to find the hidden water holes. This friend, who resided in a Mohave Desert town, paused and chuckled softly.

Then he uttered words that were as a cool drink to a parched mind . . . "You know, Sue," he said, "the mountains, they fill us up, but the desert empties us out so that we might fill again. If you look closely, you'll see there are beautiful mountains looming on the horizon."

As said, I'd always had a passion for the written word. As a child, I'd proudly hang little poems on the refrigerator door for my mother and write notes to my Gram. Only my own valentines with personal verse would do, and the daily journal in my diary was my secret treasure where truths were told. In high school, I loved the English classes. In college, I eagerly anticipated every Literature or Creative Writing course. Later, while pondering my friend's simple comment, a ray of sunlight peeked through the windows in the room behind the door numbered *Three*. Donning a new shawl of resolve, I took the first step inside.

I started writing with a vengeance. Every thought, every fear, every resentment started spilling out on papers and scratch pads. Another secret diary came to life. I began writing poems again; poems that made little or no sense to anyone but me. Sometimes, they made me laugh so I started playing around with humor and satire. Soon even the grocery list took on the flair of rhyme, silliness, or the philosophy of why to buy leafy greens.

I started buying those blank greeting cards and writing my own verses again for special people and special occasions. I played with the word processor on the computer and started writing essays. I started going to the philosophy forums on line and just reading what others had to offer. Occasionally, if a discussion aroused me enough, I'd gather some grit and post my own ideas and opinions. After all, I'd read a bit of Socrates myself!

I soon discovered interaction with like minds was what had been lacking in my life. Oh, not the face to face kind, the 'hellos' and 'how are yous'. I deal with the public in my job so there were ample daily greetings. No, it was the thinking kind of interaction. That's what was missing. My husband and I had always been blessed with the ability to converse, debate, and haggle by the hour. We'd solved, dissolved, and solved again, the age old questions of *why* and *what for* many times over in our thirty-five year marriage.

I am an Earth person, a Cosmic person. I don't believe in coincidence, luck, or random chance. I believe everything that has ever happened to me is a guided point of Star Energy provided by the Creator. How we listen, how we react, and how we choose to deal with each circumstance in our lives determines how we will live our life. Create our life, if you will.

I believe all life holds value and is an intended part of the greater life web. From the smallest beetle to the mighty oak. My always critically organized room became a maze resembling the back room stacks at the local library. Piles of papers, research results, and lists of Spiritual and Environmental websites were about to engulf me. So I started up a website of my own, dedicating it to my husband. I felt alive and with purpose again.

I'm ten years into the room behind the door numbered *Three* now. Its walls have hangings of new friends, new places. In the corner bookcase, realized dreams collect in photo albums of the Tetons, the Giant Sequoias, the mighty Pacific. More important it holds the copies of my two published books, and now an award-winning audio of my novel. The windows now have the bright yellow curtains of new experiences dressing them.

Outside, the wild critters stay close by. The squirrels line up for breakfast on the back deck, and the raccoons and the possums greet me when I arrive home at night. Inside, two old lazy cats have taken to the new room pretty well, too. The sons visit when they can and I try to make sure they can still breathe in the familiar smells of home fires burning. My cousin Jim came to stay with me a while and taught me to share my cookies and milk again. He shared his good heart and helpful hand with me in return.

Solitude must have balance, I've learned. Too much tends to make you grumpy and self-centered. Though everyone needs breathing space and think time, too much can shrivel you up. It can take the joy out and keep your walls a drab brown. Remember that, if you have a loved one or a neighbor who lives all alone. Share a little of your cookies and milk with them.

Oh, my gardens still get a good washout now and then; the occasional thunderstorm still blows through and drops a few limbs in the yard. But the sun always returns. Really, there is no lost, there is no found, only rainbows all around riding the tail of storms. You only have to open the doors. Oh, and invest in a good raincoat.

She Rises

Out and away
from debilitating despair,
out from the shadows, Into the light,
A clarity of air.

A clarity,
Filtered through the residue
of many sleepless nights,
a ponderer's sojourn
through many mindless blights.

A time when the mind-peace
tends to waiver and fade,
And the heart-wisdom grapples
To attain a survival grade.

Oft, the course that living takes
meanders far off the track.
Then lo, a simple shift in vision
can bring the rainbows back.

Words past uttered
by a high-flying friend,
wrestled through my mind-fog
To offer quiet mend . . .

"There is no lost," a soft whisper said,
"and there is no found . . .
There's really only the rainbows
gathering all around."

Deep in the dark corridors
of my tattered mind
A gentle harmony calls.
Candles of light flicker,
across my scathed mind-walls.

Rising . . . listening . . .
Hope sings over tragedy's wails
While all across the Infinite,
the Stars mark new trails.

All is well, all is well
in the Cosmic great beyond,
Things are as they should be
across this physical pond.

I smile.
Then, call to my farthest star . . .
"Just one last book, my dearest,
then I'll be with you.
I'll be with you where you are."

~ 2006 ~

Poets Rule

If you're driven to be a writer, chances are you're destined to spending a lot of time alone. Writing, especially creative writing, is a solitary venture. Rather suddenly though, you may feel just as driven to share your work with the world. I suppose we all think that what we've experienced, shared, felt or created is worth something for the eyes of the public. For most of us, this means leaving our comfort zone. For some, this departure evokes pure terror.

My first book, *Fibers in the Web*, consisted of poetry and essays. It seemed natural to think of myself as a poet. I searched for a poetry group to visit. I pondered on the slogan coined by Linda Neckel White for *Voices of Venice,* the group I chose to visit. *Poets Rule!* The group has bumper stickers and window decals proclaiming this status to the readers of the world. It was, and still is, their motto.

Just what is it that poets rule, I wondered. Poets and poetry are surely not the most well-received writers and writing style, and arguably, it's the hardest genre to sell.

I entered my first meeting a frightened little woman who, sheepishly arrived at Books a Million thirty minutes late. I'd read about the group in a publication that hadn't corrected a time change. I nervously approached the group and was warmly welcomed. In terror, yes terror, and total lack of confidence, I passed on my turn to read several times.

Inspired by the lovely poems my ears were hearing and the sincerity of the girls there, I finally mustered the courage to share a short verse. I rattled off a short poem titled *Heaven Is Coming?* And, I do mean rattled off! I knew absolutely nothing about reading my work out loud in front of people. Smiles and encouragement were freely given, though, and judgment of my simple-song pleas for the Earth was withheld.

The group, deftly led by performing poet, Linda Neckel White, extended their hands to me in support, and I grabbed hold. Linda is still leading this cherished group of friends and I'm still humbly following and learning. I have learned that reading our work is an art in itself. Linda has taught me so much and the other poets, both ladies and gentlemen, are a continuous fount of inspiration. I have learned what poets rule means, as well.

Poets Rule is, first, a slogan for a poet to feel good about their particular writing genre and themselves. Personally, the poet in me rules as it is the chosen vehicle of expression by my mind, heart and soul. It's the 'written me', that me who becomes

Sucarha, my pen name. Even my oft-written prose is laden with a poetic tempo.

Secondly, Poets Rule is a gathering, a meeting of like-minds and like-souls who relate and feel security in each other's presence. It's a weekly respite where we can peel away the facades, the costumes we wear doing what it is we do everyday. It is a few moments in the whirlwind of life in which to unwind. It's a chance, if taken, to be who and what we really are without fear of competition, rejection, and judgment. It's a sharing of higher things. I've been to many writing functions and I don't think there is any other group of like writers who admire and support each other like poets do. A poet among poets is truly a fiber in the poetry web. Competition and judgment have no place there.

Heaven Is Coming was born out of my pondering mind when thinking about the all too familiar premise that the rewards for living a good life come after our departure. Life itself is to be spent following all the rules in order to gain entry to paradise. It was triggered by a sign in front of a local church proclaiming that Heaven was, indeed, coming.

This premise always bothered me as I tend to think life, all life, is the gift and we should want to follow rules that our inner soul teaches are right; out of gratitude, not fear or quest for reward. Wyc, one of my dear poet friends in our group, has since told me she fell in love with it that first night I *rattled* it off like a magpie chattering. The words, she said, shone right through my babbling.

Heaven Is Coming?

Heaven is coming?
I find that strange.
If heaven is coming,
you mean there's a range?

Will the coming be soon?
or still far away?
Maybe next month?
Or, yet this day?

Heaven is coming?
I don't understand.
I thought I held it
in the grip of my hand.

My fingers wrapped
'round a soft colored rose.
Or, the fur of my cat
tickling my nose.

Heaven is yet coming?
Thought 'twas it that gave
the foaming white cap
to the roll of the wave.

I believed it was heaven
in the morning I hear
as the trill of a songbird
enters my ear.

But heaven is coming?
It may be a while?
I thought I'd seen it
in a small child's smile.

The sun rising brilliant
in soft morning skies,
A vision of majesty
caressing my eyes.

Oh, heaven is coming?
Am I to agree?
That this isn't heaven,
that wondrous tree?

You mean it's not heaven
that gives my heart rise
as I gaze in the blue
of a beloved's eyes?

Heaven is coming?
I shed a tear . . .
All this time,
I thought it was here.

~ 2004 ~

The Circus is Coming to Town

Even after the publishing of *Fibers In The Web*, I was still living in veritable solitude. I'd finally achieved a peace of mind. I continued to work the day job, and improve sucarha.com. The poems I wrote turned from despair-laden to pleas for the Natural world. I no longer questioned my Spirituality. A calm came to me in my thinking of the Divine as a *Force* in the world all around me. Part of a much bigger picture.

In the course of evolving, though, I became more and more aware of the ravaging our species was wreaking on the planet and the wildlife in the pursuit of our insatiable consumption. I began to really question the legitimacy of the war in Iraq and went on a quest for the justice in our method of answering the senseless destruction of 9/11. For me, there was none to be found.

Why were we so disparaged by such large portions of the globe? Was it really all about oil dominance and the dollar economy at the expense of third world countries? Was the generosity of our general population being undermined? Was the greed of the world banks and the Military-Industrial Complex, turning us into the world villain?

World History and Political Science were not my strong points at that time. I was focused on the environment and the animals. I wrote a sing-song type of poem that was really a short story.

The Circus Is Coming To Town was intended to reach children. It was to illustrate a complex problem in a simple parable that the next generation would ultimately have to deal with. We owed them some kind of education and awareness of such a crucial issue.

Circus surprisingly became a favorite poem of adults at the poetry groups I'd started to attend, so much so, that it was printed in the local newspaper in spite of its length. Folks started asking me for a copy so they could read it to their grandchildren and I ended up having it made into an E-book with illustrations.

Once it started rolling out of me, I couldn't seem to shut it off . . .

Sitting surrounded by morning's still
on the dawn-draped crest of a rolling hill,
a forest community gathered in rising mist,
their heads turned slightly in a listening twist.
A rumble in the distance was forming a frown.
Was that the Circus coming to town?

Mr. Rabbit snapped to attention,
and gathered his poise.
He wiggled his nose toward the distant noise.
"I must run now and watch over my hole.
I suggest you should also, my friend, Mr. Mole."
Off they scampered, the hill, they ran down,
hoping the Circus wouldn't come to their town.

An old black crow flew
to the very top of a tree,
a better vantage point from which to see.
On the highest branch above morning's haze,
machines belching smoke greeted his gaze.
Fear stabbed his heart, recognition, his mind,
he cawed out his warning
with all the strength he could find.

The mechanical menagerie inched
toward the knolls, earthmovers, bulldozers,
surveyors with scrolls.
The performers, the workers, saws with big chains,
mindless to the destruction, unaware of the pains.

The embarking invasion would
bring wealth of renown. A bigger, better than ever,
Circus was coming to town.
The forest residents breathed deeply
in a resigned sort of heave. The trees
seemed to shudder and fold up their leaves.

The whole forest trembled
with the pounding of feet
as they ran to their families
with news of another defeat.
The brook seemed to gurgle louder than ever before,
as if issuing warning
to the creatures who lived on its floor.

The doe fetched her baby, an amber-hued fawn,
and rustled it from hiding
for the run that would come.
The bear told her cubs, "follow closely behind,
we must hurry, quickly,
a new home we must find."

The forest was a flurry, no time to waste.
The Circus is coming.
They must leave in haste.
Soon there'd be digging and gnashing of grass,
Clearing and grubbing
for what was coming to pass.

Soon would come roads,
ribbons of asphalt and stones,
and row after row of look-alike homes.
Stores and shops and restaurants to eat,
yet, nary a place
for all the animals to meet.

Mrs. Raccoon worried
just where they'd sleep next.
The birds would be hard-pressed
in building new nests.
Mr. Possum thought sadly of his family past lost.
Small price for the Circus, but to him, a great cost.
The frogs began croaking warnings
to those of their kind, Clean water for them,
was becoming harder to find.

The trees that had lived so long standing tall,
seemed to steady their limbs to ward off the fall.
The wind calmed suddenly
as if signaling its dread,
soon only structures of brick
would stand in its stead.
No pungent fragrance of seasons,
no murmurs of wood life,
no singing of windsongs lacking in strife.

As the forest scurried
to move somewhere more right,
the rumbling moved faster, its target in sight.
In a large circle they gathered
at the base of the knolls,
The surveyors quickly began
unrolling their scrolls.
Smiles on their faces,
fingers pointing this way and that,

They began shouting orders to men in hard hats.
Soon the forest was filled
with a noisy whine.
Acrid smells overtook the odor of pine.
The Earth started moving,
growing into a black wall.
A majestic Maple, many rings in its core,
was the first tree to fall.
Before nightfall,
a great many more would be down,
The Circus was well underway
in building its town.

Off a great distance,
a coyote howled a new tune.
The wolves, they too, gathered
in the light of the moon.

Mrs. Raccoon dried her babies' tears
as she put them to bed.
One more time, they'd found
a place to lay head.
The bunnies, tired, from running
and digging new holes,
Hoped there was room enough left for the moles.

Once again settled as day faded and night fell,
of one more move, they'd lived to tell.
Yet, how many more
would they be able to make

If more and more forests, the Circus did take?
When would come the time
that there'd just be no more?
And only the Planet
could then even the score?

Diversity and beauty
are the premium life gift.
The effects of our cause
will be heavy to lift.
Try to remember
the next time you see,
death littering the roadway,
piles of dead scrub and trees.

The circus being bigger
simply may not be the way,
when the price of a ticket
is more than we can pay.
Clean water, fresh air, the scent of a tree,
are as important as living
environment rule-free.

Things have a way of needing a scheme,
a blending of nature with a sharing theme.
One day it will be people
who sit with a frown,
when distant rumbles warn
that the Circus is coming to town.

A Gentle Sea

Regardless the role that I'm writing, speaking or relaxing in, my readers and the people around me see the essence of the sea. Whether Sucarha.com, on book covers and pen names, or in Amber's comfort zones and adventures, Susan the me, living and working, there'll be references to the sea.

Earlier this year, a local magazine was featuring submissions by those of us who were lured here, lived here or dreamed of retiring here. Just what was it that attracted folks to this southwest Florida Gulfcoast? I decided to write *A Gentle Sea*. It was accepted and I decided it belongs in this book, too. The essay entwines into the life of each *ego-role* I happen to be wearing . . .

The South Florida Gulf Coast is an ambiguous world of raw nature and the attempts of human taming. The mainland is protected by a series of elongated, rather narrow barrier islands worn almost like a necklace around the neck of the peninsula.

Sugar-white sand, littered with delicate Coquina shells glistens on miles of Gulf shoreline.

Flocks of sandpipers strut, almost frantically, among the multi-hued Coquinas searching their contents for breakfast or dinner. Tiny white sand crabs timidly dart in and out of their seaside holes eluding the raucous gulls. At tide change, just off shore, the dolphin pods arc out of the water in their own display of magnificence. Sometimes they are feeding, but often they are merely engaging in play and gaiety, in their joy of life, perhaps.

In wider expanses of the island beaches, sea oats and wild daisies wave in the wind gusts, offering their own version of a Midwest prairie. The bright yellow flowers are the perfect contrast to the sugar sand, turquoise water, and azure skies. Sky, sea and sand are peppered with an abundance of seabirds who nest in the estuaries along the Intra-coastal waterway. This liquid thoroughfare ambles between barrier key and main shore like the chain of the island necklace. Along its highway shoulders, mangroves and sea grapes tangle here and there; they are protected now. A variety of fish, turtles and manatees take refuge in the arms of their shallow water roots.

The old Florida shore is struggling to survive amidst the high rises, the bustling tourist shops and boat marinas. Glass restaurants have replaced the old seaside fish shanties, but their character lingers in our memories. The Intracoastal is often congested with boats and skidoos, their oily residues wafting on the surface. The keys themselves shudder at the foray. They erode and shrink in the invasion of the vegetation that once held their sand intact. I feel the loss.

The savior of it all for me, though, is the sea. We have a soul connection, this tranquil sea and me, a kinship of spirit that melds us together within the fabric of all life. It exists in me, and me in it, yet it is the master. Perhaps that is the lure of the Gulf for many; its respite from the people noise, both its power and majesty exuded at once with its serenity. Nature's paradox, this small gentle sea.

I dwell in the little burg of Nokomis nestled between Sarasota and Venice close to the water on the mainland. In dawn's sea mist, I walk to the key and sit huddled at the shore, knees to chest, as a small roll of water unfurls at my toes. I watch the gulls play, showing no concern for my human musings.

Gazing then, far into the distance where the sky falls into the water, I feel a new wind stir the currents. The waves swell slightly, filling me with energy to begin a new day to do with what I will. Perhaps that is the lure of the Gulf, the quiet times.

Dusk brings, literally, a celebration of sunset. There is a drum ceremony three nights a week on our Casey Key shore. Assembling by the water's edge, a throng of all ages, races and theologies gather in a reverence of whatever personal spirituality they feel. They tote their bongo drums, tom-toms, old cooking pots, wooden spoons and rattles to pound out the beat of the Native American sunset dance.

A huge circle grows. We watch the sun descend while the drum rhythm builds to a crescendo of cosmic joy as the orange-red orb dances on the water. The air clarity blending with the sea fog brushes a mural of spectacular art across the heavens and the sea's fiery surface. The sun disappears below the western sphere; a day is done. You have done with it what you have. Maybe this is the lure of the Gulf, the joining of humankind and nature.

The sea, dark and endless, is an enigma at night. When sleep evades, I ride along the key road peering into the blackness that is the water. That the water is there is an absolute, but where it begins and how far it travels to the horizon is shrouded in obscurity. Yet, you can hear it, hear the rolling surf of it tumbling onto the sand, composing its own kind of symphony. Possibly it's the sea at night that lures . . . its mystery.

But, this serene sea can shed its calm and rile mightily. In the two year period of 2004 and 2005, eight powerful hurricanes entered the Gulf of Mexico, six of them preceded the unforgettable *Katrina* in 2005. When Hurricane Ivan, a massive Category 5 storm, roared north through the Gulf bearing down on the Florida Panhandle in 2004, our coast, still reeling from Hurricane Charlie's battering two weeks prior, was pummeled again with Ivan's resulting mountainous waves.

This time, however, with the eye-wall well off shore, the bridges were left open to residents. Leaning on the wind, I stood in awe of the raw power of this now angry water. I was humbled by its message of wrath, its ferocity. I pondered why humankind seems intent to build in the few areas where Nature should be unmolested, left to be what it is . . . wild and free. And protector, too. These land strips called *keys* are also intended to serve. They are defined barrier islands. Don't the developers understand the meaning of *barrier*?

I watched in sadness as the shoreline moved closer and closer to the vegetation. Several of the walk-over decks were destroyed that day. Nature must be nurtured if this planet and its resources are to continue providing us our home and our survival in this physical dimension.

I can't imagine living without this Gulf sea, or some sea, in my veins, its salt breath in my own lungs. It sings to us its songs if we'll but listen, listen like the dolphins listen as they arc up and out of the water and bow to the sun. An ocean should make us think and appreciate our place here on this earth. It should also remind us of our smallness in the big scheme of things. Maybe that is the lure of the Gulf for me . . . the joy in the attainment of a natural wisdom and humility in a world of competition, greed, and bustle. A world of noise.

A Certain Justice

Look around you. What is it that you see?
A certain justice in the way of things?
Any hints of what's yet to be?
Anything around you
triggering cause for alarm?
A certain justice owed . . .
the result of all our harm?

And why my desperation?
That's often asked of me, as well.
Is it just another thing to write about,
another thought to tell?
Tell, in the splatter of the valiant pleas
I often spill upon a page,
Imploring for a Certain Justice
for the Earth wars
Our insatiable passions wage?

Every soul has its journey,
as does the Soul of Earth.
A certain path of destiny,
a certain innate worth.

Is there a call for Certain Justice?
Is my desperation sound?
What's about to be our cost?
Is our price already found?

Yes, there is a cry for Certain Justice
from that view we see around!
From every towering redwood
and every dying creature,
just before it hits the ground!

I've pondered on this Justice rule
a good share of my life.
Often beyond reason,
spurred by my anger and my strife.

I do believe in the Higher laws,
the cause and effects of life.
What goes around must come around,
be it wrong or right!

A certain justice built right in when
God said, "Let there be light."

I Have a Dream

The Natural world had given me so much in a time when I'd so desperately needed a sense of solace and understanding; I felt an urgent need to give something back. What? I didn't know. I'd always felt at home outside of doors and walls. I'd long revered the majesty of Nature's beauty and power, its serenity in the middle of a desert, its ferocity in a hurricane or shelter in a forest.

On the many cross-country trips trucking with my husband, I'd learned something else. Though its power is ultimate in the physical dimension, its dependence on balance is crucial. Actually, Nature is a fragile world that must be diligently cared for if it is to continue to provide the variety of species which inhabit it a suitable home.

With my own eyes, I've seen the effects of drought, flash floods, the scarred mountainsides of clear cutting, and the dwindling of wildlife which provides the natural balance of the food chain. From high mountain summits, I've seen the smothering layers of smog settling over a city.

After starting to attend the poetry group, *Voices of Venice*, I was so taken with the facilitator that I began looking at poetry in a whole different way. *Linda Neckel White, in addition to being an illuminating person, is a vibrant performing poet, a poetical stage actress. Her meaningful poems have been recorded on a CD with soft-toned music playing in the background. The disc further illustrates her soul-driven words. It was Linda who inspired me to coin the reference to poems of passion as "Soul Songs."

Passion, to me is any emotion that rumbles in our very beings, the inner voices of the extreme. The passion I refer to can be fueled by fear and fury as easily as love or reverence. It is the soul of who we are and what we feel and believe.

For so long, I'd used my poetry for personal ramblings written only for my own eyes or to send a thought to another on a greeting card or note. Through Linda, I realized that poetry could be used to communicate the thoughts and ideals that gave my life purpose again. A purpose lost when my husband passed on. Poetry, with its unique brevity, can be a planter of seeds that grow a garden of thought, cheer or learning. The poet can become the cultivator. This is what I could give back to Nature.

And once again, I had a dream.

Linda Neckel White – www.poetsrule.com

I Have a Dream

I Have a Dream
Four little words, famous now,
invoked by all which exist,
if only in silence without, yet screaming within.
If only by instinct. If only to survive.
I have a dream.

A goal is a thing to achieve,
a desire to be met, a possession to attain.
But a dream is a passion,
a vision, of how things could or should be
if each human hid from their view,
the heights and demands of the culture.

Looking instead, to their reasoning, their logic,
allowing their conscience to become conscious.
If only they had ears to hear the utterings
of the crying souls that rumble
unheard in their gut
as they travel deep into the corridors of greed
and the selfishness of power.

A dying tree sheds its shriveling leaves,
like tears, on the bulldozed ground where it lies,
the saw-wound dripping its blood-sap
into the earth that bore it.

A polar bear drowning in the now warmer waters
is searching for a stability
and a meal for its young,
as baby harp seals lay battered and bloody
to be gathered for their fur while mothers lay shot,
spilling their guts onto the now, red snow . . .
I have a dream.

The sobs of a small child clutching,
with its remaining arm,
the burned bodies of its dead parents
echo on my senses.
Still, they send yet more youth
to enter this fray of insanity
to kill . . . or be killed.

I have a dream . . .
But insomnia engulfs me.

Offense

I find no offense in lust for,
but in lust against.

I find no offense in fighting for country
but in wanton destruction of life.

I find no offense in insatiable greed
for beauty in eye,
or in power, when shared with the powerless.

I find no offense in bountiful riches
If gathered in hard work and heart.

Or, in judgment's retribution
If taken on the avengers.

I find no offense in rage,
resentment, or quiet despair,
If shown in recompense.

I find love offensive
If directed only at self.

I find sport offensive if only to win
With no rules of game.

My prayer for Earth is
that it be more forgiving of us
than we've been of it.

My promise to Earth is
Reverence, first,

To its flora and fauna,
Its majestic ferocity.

Then . . . Submission
When it's time to pay the toll.

Clutter

Chaotic musings, obsessions
left lying hither and fro
on tables and chairs in my mind rooms.
Rumbling around in fog around the windows.
Lurking in the mental storms
of rage, resentment. Of quiet despair.
Clutter . . .

Reflections grow
in quiet gardens of memory.
Forgotten dreams sing from the lyrics of a song
amidst the flowers.
Love living. Death. Love discovered. Death again.
A small kitten whimpers
in the arbor by the swing.

Unbridled passions for Gaia
accompanied by birdsongs in a forest
As my mind drools on a page.
Words desperately seeking expression, a poem,
a smattering of prose, begging for compassion
not found for the wolf
who howls its agony to the moon.

The humdrum, the noise.
The noise of lives, wretched,
living with no vision beyond the darkness
of a single day.
I sit now, deafened and mind-boggled
at the insanity of the sightless seers.

I listen to the war guns
and dread the blood of youth
seeping into the soil
to feed the power lusts permeating the souls
of the man beasts.

A sigh for the dying civilization
escapes my chest.
I swipe at the tears
inching their way down my cheek,
falling into the abyss surrounding me . . .

A small kitten whimpers
in the arbor by the swing.

Clutter . . .

Mystify

Strong breezes scoop
brittle leafs from the roof.
There's a clatter, almost a rattling sound,
as in swirls, they cascade toward the ground.
It's dry, so dry, so fire-prone dry.
The weather seems to be pulling a spoof,
nary a cloud to blemish the sky.
Such lack of water to an Earth that thirsts,
tends to mystify.

In a realm of Nature
so exquisitely planned
It seems something has gone awry.
Winter is waning, but spring is waiting.
Shouldn't be this dry,
this terribly dry.

I can almost hear the trees crying in pain
as limb-stretched arms
seem to be praying for rain.
If a quenching shower doesn't come soon,
the new shoots surely will die.
Such lack of water to a tree that thirsts
really tends to mystify.

The climate is changing, the scientists warn.
Ice caps are melting, sea levels are rising
A new era of weather is surely being born.
Water that was frozen and seas that were low
are suddenly increasing in volume and flow.
So why is it so fiery dry?
It really tends to mystify.

But remember those trees
that once lined the road?
Giving rest to the eyes
from the signs and the stores?
They're gone, you see, they had to come down.
Seems they were in the way
of the developer wars.

The dust and the asphalt have taken their place.
Their heat and their grit rise into the sky.
Swallowing the rain
that might've otherwise fell
If only the trees had been left
to mystify.

Ponderings

I'm a ponderer by nature. I tend to analyze without intending to. Life's experiences have led me toward not blindly accepting the face value of anything. Things, definitely, are not always as they appear. I find that to be the case, especially, in things taught and told by others. Humans seem unable to control adding their own perception of things as they tell or pass them on. Our interpretations and perceptions are how our thinking brains work, so that is to be expected, I suppose.

Often, and to my detriment, I'll react emotionally to a situation or a comment, but invariably ponder it in detail later usually changing my mind. Or at least, have a deeper understanding of the incident. Critical thinker, I've been called. I take that as a compliment. It seems to be a lost art in today's volatile times.

Most of us have become self-centered in order to survive the chaos. We are quick to believe the worst, to fear, to hate, to judge and to expect with utmost expedience, solutions to problems regardless how long in the making, or our own part in making them. Politics comes to mind.

Being a lover of words, though, I find myself scrutinizing the words we toss around in everyday language and speaking. The dictionary is one of my favorite books. When looking up a word to verify correctness in an article or essay, more times than not I'll be attracted to the one above or below it and end up spending an hour on a tour of synonyms. It's a fascinating journey.

Bob Delany and I used to spend hours debating critical issues and emotions back and forth in emails. In that experience, I was able to somewhat replace the long conversations husband Jerry and I had while trucking coast to coast. I think, too, it was the gestation period of Amber and Ben, the building of the personalities that later became the novel, *Rainy Day People.*

Being a lover of metaphor, a deep thinker, and a scribbler of thoughts, the following are poems triggered by no more than a word caught up in my curiosity. They came in another time of loss after Bob, too, left this Earth.

What is Coincidence?

Chaos darting through the order
Like a sword through destiny?
Or the other way around?
Order molding the confusion,
Music permeating the sound.

Hapless victims of chance,
an event of good or bad?
Or is coincidence a concurrence?
an agreement with what is to be?
A molecule of water
in the tempest of life's sea?

A sorceress of mysticism?
A demon lying in obscure shadows?
A lady named Luck that dishes our fate?
For one, God's hand is outstretched?
For another, it's simply too late?

Am I to flail on wisps of my existence?
Tossed about, helpless,
in a swirl of happenstance?
No, I'm too controlling for that.

The law of attraction reigns king;
polarity its queen!
Dependent on vision, perception,
my energy of mind.
A triadic funnel of potential spins.
Circles turn, I live and I'll die.
Some days I'll crash,
some I'll fly.

But I have lived,
have trod with you . . .
on this blue Planet in the Infinite.
And, therein lies the real coincidence . . .
Think about that.
Really think about that.

Excommunicate?

What is this . . . this separation?
This denial of my existence?
My mind? My deeds?
Who, what, are you to dismiss me from my life?
My experiences . . . my consequences?
That is not your role here.
Yours is to mind to your own
existence, mind and deeds.

Sometimes, I walk this path with purpose,
head held high and strong.
Times, I crawl on bloody knees,
learning right from wrong.
My only judge in how I stand or fall
is that image staring back at me
from the mirror on the wall.

You think I don't bleed enough
when a wrong choice I have made?
Or, that I need your favor,
only when I crest a pre-set grade?
Oh, how you misjudge me
from your ivory tower of rules.
You know not what drives me on!
I need not prove myself to fools.

Mine is to be, to learn, then share.
The pitfalls I can then, perhaps others, spare.
Not shun them, judge them,
toss them off the road.
But help them, lift them,
In carrying their own load.

So excommunicate, separate,
deny me if you will.
My soul, you cannot touch,
But I will weep for you,
you've truly lost so much!

Excommunicate was written for a friend; a friend who'd been excommunicated from her church upon remarrying after obtaining a divorce from an abusive spouse. It was my own reaction to her plight.

My heart ached for her. She was allowed no chance at happiness and fulfillment? No chance for her Creator's blessings for a new life? This poem came out of an inner rage at the way of things, the boundaries placed around the Divine by a man-made doctrine.

My intent was to but lighten her sorrow, offer a new perspective. I'm happy to say she has never looked back, but searches the new horizons opened to her. Her faith in the Divine is even stronger.

Shadows

I now know beyond the shadows
that enter the valleys now and then,
like demons, trying to cast doubt on truth.
I've wallowed in enough shadows
To know them for what they are – fear.
Perhaps ignorance.
I know that a vibrating strand of energy
Connects me to that
with which I'm intended to meld.
And pulls me like a magnet
away from that
which would color my beauty into gray.
When truth pours forth through words from soul,
a vibrant strand of amber light
glistens over the valley,
twixt the shadows and connects
their light to my own.

Improper

What is proper?
Improper is but the polarity.
Here, there, in between, in all things.
We judge, perceive,
we settle, submit, justify.
We walk, live, and pay.
Bitch and do nothing.

Tragic, isn't it,
when absolute can't be defined?
When definitive is lost in gray surrender
and paranoid loyalties.

Breath

Giver of Life . . .
Sustenance
to the lung,
skin cell, gill or leaf.

Imperative,
to all aerobic phenomena,
if it is to survive.

The Earth is an aerobic phenomenon,
the trees, its lungs.
Yet, man would elevate himself,
Collectively,
above a forest?

Think about it!
If you wish to survive . . .

Turtles

In the dew of morn, I stretch
from out my little house of shell.
Sauntering slowly down my garden path,
I am startled by the quell.

The crush of hustle bustle.
the scurrying, hurrying feet,
nearly stepping on my house!
I wish they'd take a seat.

I wonder why all the mayhem?
Why don't they stop and rest?
Breathe in all the garden smells,
absorb the Nature's best?

What is the big hurry?
Why all the noise?
They trample what they're looking for
in their search for all life's joys.

I'll get where they're going.
Just maybe not as fast.
But, I'll linger in the beauty
before I breathe my last.

I hum softly to the song
of my favorite bird,
and wonder if those rushing folks
know what they've never heard?

I smile at the butterfly.
Close my ears to all the clap.
I wander 'neath the flowers,
tuck my head, and take a nap.

Flame

A nuance, a metaphor of fire
Trials by hardship, a soft glow of light
Or the blade of the torch, still leading the fight?
Flames of destruction, or fingers of warmth?
A change of energy from a log reduced to ash
The funeral pyre of a Viking's death
Or the stinging of whip's lash?

A glimmer of sparking hope
in the depth of heart and soul
when it conquers one small goal?
Or is it that principle, that never-ending need,
that old flame that's never gone,
burning the mind, searing the gut,
just what is right and what is wrong?

Thoughts on Politics
and Author Sharing

Once I'd achieved having published books *out there,* and by nature not a marketer, like many writers do I decided to write my way to a semblance of public familiarity with my work.

Other than my website and my books, I had no exposure and simply am not one to 'sell' myself or my own work. I started writing book reviews for other authors never realizing the extent it would also open doors for me.

Having had some past experience in journalism when I was at Kent State University, a good friend of mine, Lois Stern, a fellow Infinity Author became one of my most loyal advocates. After meeting at the Infinity Authors Conference, Lois had become attached to my books, my writing style and the reviews I was writing for other authors. I'd written two for her very successful books, *Sex, Lies, and Cosmetic Surgery* and *Tick Tock, Stop the Clock.*

At the time, Lois was writing a Health and Beauty column for a west coast publication to expose her own work in that field. We'd had some fiery political discussions and she encouraged me to attempt writing a political column. Of course, I told her I wasn't qualified for such an endeavor. It would be most difficult for me to remain impartial regarding content, as a good editorial journalist must be able to do.

Lois, however, is not easily deterred. That's one of the things I love about her. She gave my name and a bit of background to Yana Berlin, editor and founder of *Fabulously Forty and Beyond*. I sure met the over forty criteria!

Mrs. Berlin contacted me and asked me if I would send her a few samples of my writing. After a couple of email interviews, Yana took me on board and I wrote political columns throughout the last presidential campaign and have continued since.

I was fortunate enough to gather a readership there who, in turn, checked my profile and started buying and recommending my books without me even mentioning them. The writing sold the writing. There's a tip for new authors who may be reading this little book. One must give in order to receive.

The next selections include a whimsical essay, a personal favorite political article and three poems written during the 2008 election campaign.

A Bit of Humor

Probably next to our faith, whatever that may be, our inspirations and our personal passions, humor and the ability to laugh, especially at ourselves, feeds the soul as much as anything. I don't know of a person who, deep down, doesn't love to laugh. I admire those whose sense of humor is a paramount quality, and hold compassion for anyone lacking the will to search for the humorous facet of every seeming calamity. Even if it comes as a delayed reaction.

The lauding of rainbows has become my signature of sorts. Most who are familiar with my ramblings expect ample, if not voluminous, displays of poetry or prose that implores for an appreciation and caring for Nature and all of its critters. Or, weathering the storms of life with a good raincoat and sunglasses in their pocket. Those who've read *Rainy Day People*, know that although the fruit inside is of a serious fare, that the protagonist, Amber, is a bit of a quirky nut with a tendency toward mishap in which to embroil herself. Most, too, know that Amber is none other than this writer.

The recent gathering of Infinity Authors at Valley Forge and my subsequent jaunt to New York City provided many opportunities to attract trouble, as well as a lot of rainbow searching. I should've gotten my first clue the week prior to my departure from Florida. My MS Word program, somehow knowing that it held all the preparatory documents needed for my big debut as an Author Panelist, decided to malfunction. Luckily, I'd duplicated much of the needed materials to PDF files and was able to muddle through.

The day before I was to leave, I packed and loaded my silver Eclipse Spyder with everything but needed gasoline. At 6 a.m., after attempting to convince my two cats I was not abandoning them to a neighbor forever, I embarked on my three week, 4000 mile trek north via the gas station where the price had risen eight cents overnight.

After a couple of days of wandering around forests and cow pastures at the farm in North Carolina, reuniting with old friends and memories, Spirit rejuvenated, I shed a temporary lapse into a southern drawl, donned my author lapel button, and headed north for Pennsylvania and points beyond. Eleven hours later, I arrived at the home of my son in Harrisburg without incident, for Amber, a feat in itself.

Lounging, sight-seeing, and driving my daughter-in-law loony practicing my speech filled the next four days and soon I was merging onto the Pennsylvania Turnpike headed for Valley Forge. Having viewed the Liberty Bell on a previous trip, when I discovered, thanks to a wrong turn exiting the Turnpike that I was headed toward downtown Philadelphia, I drug out the infernal cell phone and called my son for a course adjustment. He knows to stay close to the device when mother is loose on the highways. Another subtle hint of what lay ahead?

That evening following more reunions with friends, my fellow authors and I had the good fortune of doing a run through of our panel presentation with dear Jerry Simmons of Time Warner fame, offering his guidance.

I quickly learned that for one who becomes paralyzed with fear at the very thought of public speaking, I'd driven my daughter-in-law loony for nothing. The time frame was reiterated and, no, I wouldn't be granted extra time to have a heart attack. But, Jerry, 'rainbow' that he is, took me under his wing. I'm proud to announce that Friday afternoon, I did my part in just under the five minute limit mark. Our moderator, dear Melanie Rigney, editor extraordinaire, carefully guarded the time with her stopwatch. Going over resulted in her sweet voice singing out, "Excuse me, time's up!"

Sunday brought an end to another incredible Infinity Publishing Conference, and me again heading west to Harrisburg to regroup for the long awaited event in New York City the following Saturday. The book signing in East Village had been promoted and anticipated for months! My son was to accompany me, the necessary reservations and itineraries were in place, so nothing could go awry? Right? Wrong.

An urgent cell phone call on Friday morning announced that due to an emergency, *New Voices* bookstore had to close. My signing had been canceled. What?! You're not serious! They were.

Instant despair invaded my being. Disappointment threatened to render me ill. I wouldn't even get the chance to fail! But, here we were, the car already again headed north. Bill has inherited the wanderlust and venturesome genes of his parents. We decided to continue on, determined to go on a rainbow hunt in the midst of the storm. Author button secured on lapel, book bag and flyers ready, I'd make sure New York knew of my existence. Somehow!

We checked in our hotel, freshened up and headed to the Amtrak train at Newark airport and boarded the next train into the *Big Apple*. Bill was familiar with the city, but although I'd been all over New York State, it was my first trip to Manhattan. I hung on for dear life as he pulled me through the hordes at Penn Station.

We purchased a three day tour bus pass and began our hunt. Every notable landmark was visited. On the Saturday Night Light tour, the tour guide, always looking for a comic gimmick to liven the crowd, fixed his eyes on my Author button. Suffice it to say here, the *rainbow* appeared big time. I now know why Brian Judd touts *Beyond the Bookstore*!

Exiting the bus at Central Park and 58th Street, we prepared to walk back to 34th and 7th Avenue – Times Square. I then learned why there's a drug store on every corner in the city. They're first-aid stations. A row of horse drawn carriages along the perimeter of the park drew me like a magnet. To hug a horse after being surrounded by humanity for two days would be the ultimate end of a wonderful day. Wouldn't it? No.

The horse decided my finger resembled a carrot and seconds later my son was furiously attempting to halt the flow of blood exiting my body through a severed artery. Not the way I intended leaving my *mark* on New York! Refusing assistance from New York's finest much to Bill's dismay, he performed minor surgery on the sidewalk outside the corner drugstore. An energizing cappuccino was obtained at the Columbus Circle Starbucks, and we started on the twenty-four block hike south, me in a swath of bandages and butterfly closures.

Hobbling into the throngs on the Square, my ankle was immediately stomped on by someone weighing at least a thousand pounds and staring up at the plethora of modern digital advertising. Now, injured in two extremities, my son decided the casualties were again mounting against us and it was time to get mother off the streets.

The next morning we headed back to Harrisburg as my walking tours were over. Upon arrival in the garage and exiting the vehicle, I was immediately struck on the forehead by a piece of lumber disturbed at the vibration of the garage door opener and breaking free of its perch in the rafters. Once more, I was seeing lights rivaling those of Times Square, and blood was again exiting my body from a lump that would balloon to the size of a golf ball.

Son Bill is totally convinced his mother is an accident in search of a place to occur, and beginning to worry about her 1500 mile return trip to Florida that was to commence the next morning. I told him not to fear. I had a couple of really good co-pilots. He smiled, knowing that I was referring to his dad and my own.

I think by this time, my dear daughter-in-law, Karen, is thoroughly convinced that her marrying into a family with a history of mental disorder is a distinct possibility.

I arrived home three days later, horse bitten finger still encased in bandages, a black eye, an ankle with a striking resemblance to a football, and a grateful heart for my three days as a "New Yorker". My neighbor looked at me aghast, and inquired if I'd been in an accident.

"Nah", I answered, "just a few battle scars from my latest rainbow hunt. The last 600 miles were the hardest. How's my cats?"

Following, is one of the political columns written for *Fabulously 40* in the summer of 2008. The examples included are old news now, but the tenets being written never change. All one must do is change the few examples given.

How Much Do We Want to Know?

Freedom of Expression has always been the foundation, the very backbone, of the American Ideal. It's the *right* most lauded in dissertations on the unique and powerful structure a democratic form of government affords the people. It's what sets democracy apart from all other forms of rule, this freedom to express. It's guaranteed in the Constitution with an array of inclusions: freedom of speech, freedom of the press, freedom to worship as one chooses, freedom to bear arms, and freedom to vote. All are forms of individual expression.

Obviously, due to the innate idiosyncrasies of most human beings, this much 'freedom' could lead to chaos! Hence, we must enact a myriad of laws to temper the more robust expressions, you know, like guidelines not to cross. In turn, this creates a whole profession of legal minds required to interpret infractions falling somewhere between the *right* and the *line not to cross.* This then, gives birth to yet another huge system of judiciary to monitor the deliberations of alleged infractions. Aaah, only in America!

For the purpose of this column, however, I'll focus on freedom of the press, or now more aptly called, freedom of the media. Rather than exploring the realm between the right to express and the forbidden line not to cross, I propose an implementation of that oft-forgotten guideline called *common sense*. Sure, the people have a *right* to know, but how much do they need to know? Do they even care? Should the right to know obliterate the responsibility of the news to dispense pertinent information? Should sensationalism override relevance? Should circulation or ratings circumvent consequence?

This past week, I was hoping that in the break afforded us by the running of the Olympics, we'd have a respite from the negative. We'd get to witness the inspiration, the dedication, and triumph of the human spirit in intense competition but guided by mutual respect of endeavor. We'd witness the world coming together in a unity of humankind. I literally craved the positive energy that would be the result.

Now, I have to wonder, cynic that I've become, why the timing of the announcement of Senator Edward's adulterous betrayal? Why on the very day of opening ceremonies in Beijing? Why the escalation of tension in the former Soviet nation of Georgia at this precise time? Why so much emphasis on what the Chinese have done wrong in the hosting of the Olympics rather than the monstrous effort they've put forth? Why are negative campaign ads being run on the breaks when millions are watching? Is there anything that political power and money cannot buy?

Do I want to know, or even care, if Edwards' lapse into immorality is as, or more, devastating than John McCain's or Bill Clinton's, or any other plethora of public figures'? Frankly, there simply isn't anything new here! It's been going on since Alexander the Great! Politicians, no matter how capable or astute in their aspirations of public service, do not rise above their humanity into sainthood upon election. If as much emphasis were put on the exposure of underhanded dealings in the halls of Congress and the backrooms of the White House, not to mention the Supreme Court, the treasury and the Fed, perhaps I'd want to know more. But, it seems information of that nature, if it comes out at all, comes years after the event when not much can be done about it.

This is not to say the public shouldn't be informed of these behaviors, especially if public funds or donations are involved, but do we need the almost non-stop analysis by pundits and fellows who might not be so lily pure themselves? Report it, yes. Demand an accounting, yes. Store it for future decision making, yes. But then move on! I want to know about the policies being put forth on energy independence and the economy. I want to hear the pros and cons in discernable debate, not negative attack sound-bytes and empty rhetoric. I want to know what policies the candidates propose in the achievement of a calm in the world when another potential war zone is about to erupt! John Edward's love life just doesn't seem that crucial to me right now. My sympathies are with his family and their *right* to privacy. The prognosis of his future political chances doesn't mean squat to me. Dancing usually demands payment to the fiddler, as it should.

I don't know about you, but I don't want to hear some jerk's evaluation of Mr. Obama's choice of vacation destination, either. I don't want to hear why he should have stayed in the states. Have we all really forgotten that Hawaii is a state in our more perfect Union? That Mr. Obama was born and pretty much raised there? That his grandmother lives there and is no longer able to travel? Frankly, if we've forgotten, or didn't know, that Hawaii is a state, or folks like to visit their grandmothers, perhaps we shouldn't be allowed to cast a vote that could affect national policy! Don't voters have a responsibility to be somewhat cognizant of these things?

I'm sure all of you could think of many more pet peeves in the pursuit of freedom of expression. Here, I'd only request that we, as recipients of this barrage, analyze for ourselves just what is relevant and what the spewed information will mean to the future of our country, our own lives, and the lives of our progeny. When does information become sensationalism and diversion from the significant? Meanwhile, for a few more days I'm going to focus on the great achievements, the positive energy, and the promise of our Planet's youth in the arenas in Beijing. They are the future of the world!

The three poems that follow were inspired during the campaign or by the results of the election. Their content shines a light on my political preferences, but they did not appear in my column. There I did make a supreme effort to maintain a nonpartisanship voice. As a lover of Nature and a detester of war, I could support no other at the time.

For What Price?

For what price do you sell your soul,
spew the remnants of your integrity
into your desires?
What sacrifice are you willing to make
in the quest of your ambition?
How many facets of naked truth
are you willing to forsake?

For what price do you harden your heart,
slash the tendons of decency
to their very core?
How many assaults of character will you employ
on others, on your own,
to mount your perceived,
your errantly due, throne?

Can the dank walls of a prison
rot away one's conscience
one tendril of worth at a time?
Does survival turn into a quiet madness
that oozes into the ego
at each small subsequent achievement?
Better to die there, or aspire to be a simple farmer.

No quest, no attainment justifies
obliteration of principle, or truth.
There is no mighty reward
or given due for choices made.
Wisdom would submit to a lowlier goal.
No accolade or earthly throne is worth
surrender of your soul.

Yes! We Can!

Sitting by the shore knees to chest
despondent, defeated,
in my cries for Earth and Nation
A small roll of water
Unfurls at my toes, humming,
an almost quiet remnant of the surf roar.
What might have been
had I not been sleeping on the sand, oblivious?
I could have . . . I should have . . .

Pondering in cool morning mist,
I watch the gulls play
without concern for my
human musings of hopelessness.
They know not, that their own survival
invades my thoughts.
They don't know of separation and turmoil,
of apathy and surrender, of the silent voices
as they chatter noisily.
They can! They never doubted that they can.
.

One or a thousand of us,
like the seabirds,
shouting in a tumultuous cacophony
against the war cries, the fear, the impossibilities
will fade in the chorus

of change, of achievement and courage.
Unless we shout louder!
Then, we can.

Peering then, far into the horizon,
I watch a new wind stir the water,
the currents swelling the waves, rising taller.
A froth of energy is bursting forth
in the white spray,
Turning into a melody . . . We can. Yes, we can.

We can, you sitting there huddled,
and all those willing to disrobe
the masks, the costumes, the anger misdirected.
Peel away the errant notions
that you're a victim and voiceless
when really, you are surrendering.

Hark, who is that singing?
That song rising to a chorus?
Yes we can. I hear the words now . . . Yes we can!
A new tidal wave crashes on the shore
of indifference and hopelessness.
Yes! We CAN!

Where Eagles Dare

Few go there . . .
high, where eagles dare.
Few can.
Few even yearn to soar
above cold and barren canyons.
Few are able to see
the menacing rodents
prey on the lesser.

Few desire to ascend
the treacherous peaks
of the hawk's lair.
Few embody the courage
to conquer the killing fields
or disturb the viper under a rock.

The broken wing of fear
encases them
in a cast of complacency.
The timidity of voice,
their distaste for criticism,
drives for acceptance into the flock.
It imprisons them in mediocrity.
Their weakness of character
reflects in their wading pools.

Enter a man,
lured by the updraft . . .
feathered in the wings of an eagles flight.
We watch, we pray, however we pray,
as he launches toward the heights . . .
where only eagles dare.

Amber

The innate love of books must come from my English genes. Remember in the old English movies how guests were always escorted by the butler to wait in the library? As I write these words, I hear the refined accent of the English butlers who often spent their lifetimes as house managers for the well-to-do.

As a child, I was an avid reader. I knew *The Bobsey Twins* series by heart, I think. By ten, Louisa May Alcott's *Little Women* carried me to another place and time. I was enthralled by Jo, the feisty, non-conformist of the four sisters. I didn't have a sister or brother then. Books allowed me to travel to other places and times, be other people and have a big loving family. The wanderlust had been born.

When I was twelve or so, the young adult books for girls began to bore me. I turned to my mother's bookshelves. One book drew me before my eyes could even focus on it. It was as if my hand was being drawn to it, *Forever Amber* by Kathleen Winsor. Amber herself, seemed to be calling to me from within the yellowed pages. Better yet, it was set in old London, before the infamous plague. A sense of *déjà vu* was suddenly enveloping me.

I devoured the book voraciously. I was in awe of Amber St. Clare, and too young to really comprehend the more risqué parts. I was struck by Amber's sense of adventure, and determination. Her courage and fortitude during the horrors of the great plague and the London fire wrenched at my depths. These and her loyalty and deep love for Bruce were written with a passion and eloquence I couldn't even totally grasp at the time. *Forever Amber* taught me the very fine line between fact and fiction and girl and woman. Winsor was a powerful storyteller.

I was surprised to learn years later, that *Forever Amber* was the *Peyton Place* of the forties. Both were banned by the Catholic Church. These days, Grace Metalias and Kathleen Winsor would both be considered dull and stodgy.

But, I'd connected with the character and vowed that I would name my first daughter Amber. I never had a daughter so I christened my inner self, my alter-ego, my very soul, Amber. Oh, and my auburn-furred tiger cat, she's named Amber, too. And of course, as it is no longer a secret, Amber also took my role in my first novel, that was really a memoir, *Rainy Day People.* Where there is a will, there is a way. Always.

A girl in our poetry group asked me to write a poem about my spirit Amber. She'd just finished reading my novel and was taken by this quirky character who she knew was me. Try as I might, I couldn't get a poem out of it. It was as if Amber demanded prose. Albeit poetically structured as it defies grammar, much of my writing does, this is what fell on the page . . .

Amber, a rather non-evasive hue. Not stark or boldly sanguine, but soft, comforting in its earthiness. It settles, surrounding in an essence you, nor I, are quite sure of. Amber is the mineral, the stone for what it is that will accept me and sculpt me into something worthy.

The color of my spirit is a golden brush that slides elusively into the shadows purveying its light into the darkness when what I am hides there.

There in the darkness, with golden ray it surrounds and embraces me with strong tawny arms, and lifts me from the nothing that I am into what I was meant to be.

I gave my efforts to my poet friend and I guess she was somewhat taken aback. She looked at me kind of funny, which in itself isn't new for me, but then her eyes watered up and tears spilled onto her cheeks. She never did explain that. I didn't push.

Making Dreams Come True

For many years now, I've been an avid believer in the old quote by Albert Einstein, "Imagination is the beginning of Creation." I've also seen this quoted as, "Imagination is more important than knowledge." Which version of the genius of Einstein is accurate, I'm not sure, perhaps both are. Both suffice to serve as the foundation of my belief.

When I began writing my novel, *Rainy Day People*, I'd decided to use the fiction genre for the purposes of embellishing certain events to make it a better story. I didn't feel anyone would be interested in reading a memoir by 'who?' The only possibility would be to wrap it in fiction and tie it with some ribbons of suspense and romance to, hopefully, develop a page turner.

Poetry and non-fiction were my only areas of writing experience, the only genres I could pour my passions on a page. I soon discovered that creating a fiction novel was beyond my present ability. I write from the very guts and soul of me and my admiration for purist creative writers snowballed!

About to admit defeat and go with the memoir, I was blessed to meet my mentor, Robert Delany, in a Spirituality and Philosophy forum on the Internet. Bob was a professional writer and taught creative writing in the adult education program at UCLA.

In the course of our discussions, our mutual love for the craft of writing was bound to come up. It wasn't long before I was telling him of my quandary and he was educating me on the required elements of fiction writing. "Mastering dialogue is the key," he said. I'd never written back and forth dialogue in my life!

For the purpose of brevity here, I'll just say it wasn't long before discussion forums turned into emails, then phone calls, and then coast to coast visits. We were a continent apart, Bob in LA and me on the Gulf coast of South Florida! Bob became a dear friend and I so adored his 'mind'. To me, he was brilliant. It wasn't too long before my fiction novel started coming together.

The dual protagonists became Amber and Ben and I created Ben from the personalities and stories of his life Bob so eloquently shared with me. I was now able to 'create' my fiction story from the necessities of my writing ability. From my own experiences and my own heart.

I wrote the following recap after Maine became a reality. The imagination theory had worked again!

Amber Returns to Maine

Will you ever revisit the cliff house, the bird cove, or again fly the silver spirit car over the coast road? Will you ever return to Maine? Is a sequel about the *Rainy Day People* on the horizon, or did Amber and Ben really find their sun? Surely, those quirky characters have another story in them! Several times, I've been asked these kinds of questions by people who've read Amber's story and became rather attached to her idiosyncratic nature. Even Ben, in his crotchety way, was endearing to my readers. I've been touched by these reactions to this peculiar pair as that is how Amber came to be. I truly felt she had a story to tell.

Family, friends, people that knew me at all, caught on pretty fast to Amber's role as protagonist. Others, of course, didn't since the book was classified as fiction and the author was relatively unknown and remains so. In reality, the story was but embellished. The characters were genuine; the sequence of events, for the most part, true. Only the Maine locale was created in the realm of pure imagination. The initial journey to the harbor town was taken by Amber. I was but the recorder of her reflective musings. On the recent return, the roles reversed. It was Amber who reveled in the events of my own trip to the North Country. Ben now rides a rainbow, so another sequel wouldn't be the same unless totally created. That won't work for me.

Earlier this year, as most of you know, a paralyzing stroke erected a road block in my meanderings. I was fortunate, and movement slowly returned to my left limbs. Nonetheless, it was a wake up call. I still had a few dreams to fulfill. It had already been arranged that when travel was again feasible, I'd go to Pennsylvania for a two month sabbatical with my son, the younger, and daughter-in-law, and of course, my granpup, BB McPup. Possibly you've read BB's stories on sucarha.com. My son, the older, was laid off work in Chicago and agreed to come to the Florida tree house and watch over the grounds and tend to the cats and critters.

In July, my younger son called from Harrisburg and in his exaggerated southern drawl said, "Hey, Maw. How'd ya like to go to Maine?"

When I chose Maine for the final setting in *Rainy Day People*, I'd never been there. It was the one missing link in my childhood dream to see the country's majesty as it was when the flag wore forty-eight stars. I'd spanned the country coast to coast and border to border as co-pilot in my husband's eighteen wheeler, but never Maine. Perhaps, it was because Maine was like the cowlick on the head of America's land face. It sort of stuck out up there in solitude, untrespassed by the major routes elsewhere. Maine held a mystery for me, a fantasy of sorts, and Amber had been my way to go; she had been my way to fulfill the creative conjuring of youth. On the last Sunday of August 2009, the silver convertible once again headed north. It was once again packed to capacity sans the lamp protruding from the rear window. Ben, this time, rode in the memories. In my mind's eye, I could see him smiling his fiendish grin from the passenger seat.

Upon arrival in Harrisburg, true to 'our' nature, Amber's and my wanderlust had blossomed with new life. BB McPup welcomed me heartily and assured me he'd fill Taggie's prior role. How could Amber travel to Maine without the company of a beloved rescued critter? But first, a train ride to NYC and a weekend with Lois and Ken Stern on Long Island had been planned. The click-clack of train wheels chattering on the tracks lulled me into reverie. Lois and I have become dear friends since meeting at the Infinity Publishing Conference at Valley Forge in 2006. The visit was wonderful, and this time, I left New York unscathed by the battles of Times Square unlike my first visit there with my son.

The following Friday, we all journeyed to Michigan to see my sister and her family. I was being chauffeured, perched in the back seat with BB and relaxing in the songs of moving tires on the road again. My eyes took in the beginning hues of fall on the ridgelines supporting the huge windmills of the wind farms. My spirit soared at the sight of the huge blades furiously spinning in the currents, a new experience. In the valley, a lone wooden windmill from earlier times still pumped water into the cattle troughs. Nostalgic and exhilarating at once, this scene.

The time in Michigan was another treasure to be absorbed. It was gift wrapped in hugs, laughter and continual banter. I do believe BB McPup and their family dog, Annabelle, were the stars of the gathering, though. Yani the cat, disgusted by the furor, brought back memories of Tag. Taggie would've been wrestling with the dogs rather than watching in disdain from behind the chair. Time passed too quickly and Sunday afternoon, after a chase to convince BB we wouldn't leave without him, we left my waving family in their driveway and turned toward the Interstate.

Tears clouded my eyes, and I swear I noticed a glistening in McPup's eyes, too. It's not easy to leave those we love, or to lose them when they go on before us. The tears spilled over and slid down my cheeks. The physical absence of family members now gone kind of yells at me at such family reunions, yet they continue to fill the room in essence and reminiscence.

Prior to the invitation to travel to Maine, I'd registered to attend the Tenth Infinity Publishing Conference. Writers, like truck drivers, cops, and firefighters, tend to form somewhat closed communities. Inspiration is a needed element in this writing work and these annual reunions of camaraderie rarely fail to supply it. The air fairly crackles with excitement as we see old friends and comrades and share the latest trends in the writing world. We learn and we teach, and most importantly, support, even if but for a few days. Networking it's called, and no writer can know success at any level without it in these times of rapidity and change in the way of doing things.

There are absolutes in how to network successfully. At their conference, Infinity does it well. For three days the last weekend of September, every writer present is a star and a professional whether they recognize it or not, first time author or best seller. There is no separation between the pros and the novices. Mingling is a given, and one can't help but leave with a new energy. Every writer is unique just as every person is unique. Arrogance and self-centeredness can be a writer's demise, especially in the company of other writers. Always be as good at listening with sincere interest as you are at speaking and self-promoting. Remember that and you'll be rewarded.

We left Valley Forge fulfilled and my thoughts turned north to Maine. We were preparing to leave the coming Friday morning. It was time to repack the bags I'd been living out of for a month.

Fittingly, Friday dawned with a cerulean mural overhead and a chill hiding in the wind. Even though I was again nested in the rear of the vehicle with my granpup, Amber was bubbling to the surface from within. The pull of her influence on me is remarkable. I'll be eternally grateful to my kids for inviting her to become my life again. I cast a loving glance toward them in the front seats. BB's thoughts, I suspected, drifted back a couple of weeks to his visit with Annabelle and his 'peoples' family. Little did he know he was about to embark on a journey across a time dimension and into the business of living a dream.

I nestled into my seat trembling with eagerness. It wasn't long before my eyes again rested on the increasingly colorful woodlands of Connecticut. Amber was returning to Maine! I sighed, audibly I'm sure, as I left this world and crossed back into the realm where only imagination can take us. I could almost smell the frost on the pumpkins once again.

Somewhere in Massachusetts, we stopped for the night. While my son unloaded his bicycles from the rear carrier and daughter went in to unlock and inspect our room, McPup and I wandered a bit into the woodline backing up to the parking area. His nose wiggled relentlessly as he darted in circles of excitement just as Taggie had done on journeys past. My heart intermittingly pounded and stopped. Some emotions are impossible to describe with semantics, even if employing the art of the metaphor I so love. It's an inner sense more than an outward feeling. I slept soundly with visions of cliff houses and surf crashing on the rocks below.

In the afternoon of the new day after wrenching through New Hampshire's mountains, I saw it. Again, I yelled out, "There it is!"

There, just forty or fifty feet ahead of us, almost hidden in the vegetation, a faded carved-wood sign announced . . . *Welcome to Maine.*

Son Bill had managed to procure us a cottage in the wilderness that was strikingly similar in structure to the cliff house. It was, however, on the shore of Echo Lake rather than a cliff by the sea. Amber didn't care; we were in a state of near ecstasy just being in Maine. We were surrounded by trees and rocky slopes a mile or so down a gravel road that was the driveway to our dwelling. I could smell the sea just over the ridge. I climbed down out of the vehicle, colliding with McPup who had the same idea. Neither of us knew which direction to go first. It was a joy unparalleled to step onto the earthy surface of Maine, breathe in the fragrances of a dream. Again, there's no language to describe the inner senses adequately.

It would require another book to reiterate the activities of the next week. I can only delve into high points, themselves difficult to prioritize, so I'll share the relative highest. The next morning, we drove to the edge of the continent, just a few miles by highway to the accessible view that I yearned for, the view I'd written in the story. I knew it was there, and I'd know it when I saw it . . .

The highway was rising now, and twisting to flow with the land's edge. The persistent pounding surf chiseled indiscriminately into the rock coastline, determined to claim for its own whatever would give way. At one point near the top, the road tunneled through the rock. Upon clearing the rock burrow, stretched before us lay the open expanse of the Atlantic. Wild sky and rolling forests adorned the cliffs framing the water. Angry water.

The splendor enclosed me, the smell, the sound, the raw power of the sea. The distant surface was a slate gray blending into blue-green pipelines that rolled in to crash against the cliffs sending giant plumes of spray high into the windswept air. Amber had come home! And this time, she brought me with her. The invisible line between character and author had finally disintegrated. Amber and Susan were once again together in Maine.

"There it is! The sea, Ben, the sea . . ."

A tear slid down my cheek as the seagull pendant, still around my neck, absorbed the cold of the wind.

What is time? It can dwell in a bottle or a river, fly or inch over a stone at a snail's pace. A slug, leaving trails like the shimmering goo of memories stored in mind rooms, cherished, denied, or guarded by locked doors.

But what is a memory? Perhaps, it's also a dimension, or fragments measuring our lives and deaths that can be revisited in reflection or present reality many times over. What are these things we call life, death, truth, and fantasy? Is there such a thing as time, really? Or but facets of dreams and imaginings of what was, is, and what could still be?

Connections or Coincidence?

I've peppered this particular book with a smathering of names of those that have influenced great shifts in my, or I should say *our* paths, Amber's, Sucarha's and mine. There are many more. The problem I run into when I attempt to give credit to all those dear to me is the list grows so tall, it becomes the book. Other than tributes to my grandmother and Papa, I'm focusing here on the years since writing has become my life.

Russ and Lee Heitz come to mind. Russ has been my *right hand* in the organizing of our local Florida Writers Association chapter. Together with his wife Lee, they've become extended family.

There are two, however, who are a story in themselves. They can't be left out or a portion of me and Amber would be left out. One has been with me since my crossing the threshold through my doorway numbered three.

I met Kathy Killam only a day or two after I entered Cyberspace. I'd been widowed a couple of weeks. Kathy had the same service provider that I had and was putting some time into a provider chatroom, rather like a welcome room for new users. Kathy was the one that started talking to me. From that day over ten years ago until now, Kathy has been there for me. If not for her, there wouldn't be a Sucarha.com, a coffee table book called *Fibers In The Web*, an e-book called *The Circus Is Coming to Town*, or a marketing program for *Rainy Day People* and its audio counterpart.

Kathy lives in Denver, Colorado and I live in Florida. What would be the chances of us forming a lifelong working relationship and friendship by pure coincidence? We've since visited in person many times and in 2001 even took a vacation tour of the National Parks west of the Mississippi. I'd say that meeting wanders into the realm of connecting with destiny. I've never written a poem specifically for Kathy. For us, the website is our poem.

In that same time frame early on in my life as Sucarha, I was also blessed by my guardian angel. I call him that because to me, he is. Tom Swain entered my life with the computer ID of *Zaotom*. Suffice it to say, he was my impetus in Spiritual understanding. Calm and collected, Tom became like my personal guru of sorts. He always had the time and the right words when I was at my lowest ebb even though we, too, lived in the three hour time gap of east and west. Tom lives in Sonoma, California. He was the first to take me into a forest of Giant Sequoias. That forest taught me more about life than fifty-eight years of living it had.

Often, he would write me a simple poem that would clarify both the cause and effect of this thing called healing. When I reached a level of absorption, I wrote a poem for him.

Zaotom, An Angel

Angels are oft thought of as purely
Spiritual Beings, Dimensional Guardians,
or a supernatural spirit riding on our shoulder
assigned to be our personal guide
whispering messages in our ear.
And these, they may possibly be.

Yet, once or twice during our journey in this
physical realm we may encounter a fellow traveler
in this fleshly abode. One that, seemingly by
chance, appears on our path and walks with us.
One that fills an emptiness, or is a buttress in our
pain. One that voices answers to the questions
confusing our heart and opens up the doorways of
new thought and ascension.

One that offers encouragement and hope in times
of struggle, loss of direction, and
one that shares laughter
when all just becomes somewhat ridiculous.
This soul has chosen to be incarnated
in the material world
only to serve others, to offer a hand . . .

A human 'Angel'.
The term "soul mate" is commonly used
in reference to romantic or conjugal relationships.
For me, soul mate has come to mean
that person who is my Angel,
Zaotom.

As you experience your journey
through this dimension,
be continually aware.
You may just meet an angel,
you may even become one.

Today, I think of Tom as my brother as well as my angel. Even now, when I'm really blue, or he is, something moves one of us to make contact. Coincidence? I don't think so.

We still talk and write and I make the occasional trip to the *Valley of the Moon*. Last year, we returned together to the redwoods taking with us a special gift. As he'd been on my shoulder when Jerry's ashes were taken to our special forest in North Carolina, I was able to be by his side when we took the ashes of Tom's life partner, Larry, to their special forest. Both of us take some comfort that we've given back to the trees what was given to us in this earthly realm. The partners that were our life.

As we get older and our psychological needs and energy levels wane, often someone will come into our lives in latter days.

The person may be unconsciously searching for an endtime friend and a connection is made. Not a coincidence at all in my way of thinking. There are just certain times when only this one person can relate to our older eccentricities on a nearly day-in day out basis.

This later-life friendship is of as much value as the ones which endure for decades. That is the way the friendship between Dahris Clair and me came to be.

Nearly five years ago, Dahris and I both entered the writing world of the Florida Writers Association. We had both just taken the challenge to become group leaders in our respective counties; her in Pasco, and me in Sarasota. It was she and I that just happened to come in together with like goals, even though there were three other counties closer to both of us who also had FWA groups. Coincidence? No we were too perfectly matched. Each brought in a strength the other didn't have. When times erupt for either of us, the other is there with strength in that which we are lacking.

After I'd known Dahris for a while, she called me one afternoon all upset because she couldn't sing anymore. She was having one of those days we all have, '*a pity party, bash Dahris*' kind of day. I didn't quite know what to say at the time. I think I just kept mumbling disagreement. Later, like always, I had a delayed reaction and wrote Dahris a poem.

It Matters Not

It matters not that your voice
trembles a bit when you speak,
but that your soul yet sings music,
music, that colors bright the otherwise bleak.

It matters not what color your hair,
the size of your dress,
or what color shoes
that you wear.

Could've beens or should've beens
are of no consequence now.
The turns in your life wrote the character
to which I humbly bow.

What matters is the determination, the fervor,
you unfailingly display
as you still pursue dreams
with vigor, afresh, day after day.

These are the things
that are of matter to me.
Not all the things that you think
you should, or must, be.

You know, God doesn't give gifts,
then take them away.
He merely changes their direction,
the role that they play.

Once you sang lengthy arias
that filled the air
with beauty and harmony . . .
a celebrity's flair.

Now you write words
from the depth of your Being
Words that might teach, soothe,
draw a tear, perhaps even sting.

But, it matters not, oh dear one,
how your soul sings its song.
Whether your choices in life
were right, or if they were wrong.

What matters is that you're made of the dust
of a faraway star.
And, you've lived your life giving
from the core of what you are.

You are a light . . .
yes, born of a star.
You've traveled a long, arduous journey
to be what you are.

So hold your head high
and let your heart sing!
So what if it trembles,
or doesn't quite ring?

The light that you're shining
is the real 'you' lighting the way.
The gift that God gave you, He never took away.
It wasn't a voice to sing or speak soundly,
but what it IS that you say.

No, I don't believe in coincidence. I believe connections are the spiritual equal to cause and effect in the physical realm. We all get them, these connections. That's the spiritual action. Whether we recognize them as such and nurture them, or write it off as coincidence is the reaction.

What does it matter, you ask? Too many of us use the coincidence concept to relieve ourselves of any responsibility for what happens. Or doesn't. Personally, I prefer to be more in control of my destiny than that.

Carla, My Sister

I've made many allusions to my sister through the years of writing. She appeared in Rainy Day People when I told the story of the rainbows. And again, in the story of Amber's return to Maine. Carla has always carried somewhat of an essence in my poems as she, along with Gram, had and still has, a profound effect on the roadways of my life and how they twist and turn. In this book, I want to formally share with the world who and what she is and means to me.

After thirteen years as an only child, my life was to take a big turn. This little wisp of life came into being with a shared blood running through her veins. We were both born with the same ancestral genetics and the spirited nature of the Aquarian. I couldn't have been more enthralled. I adored Carla with every ounce of my being. It was as if she were my baby, born for me. I didn't even comprehend sibling rivalry. I finally had a baby sister, one to share my life with.

I wanted to take her everywhere with me, and did as much as allowed. I can still see my mom's face when I would refuse to push Carla in a stroller on a walk around. Mom would shake her head wearing a confused look, but gave in. I think she knew I would never let any harm befall my sister. I'd walk off with Carla riding my hip and donning her precious baby smile as I clutched her close to me. She'd point her little finger this way and that making gurgling noises as I showed her the world around us. I vowed this treasured child would never feel unloved or unworthy as long as I drew breath.

With an age gap of thirteen years, it was inevitable that I would leave home before she was grown, but, I still took her with me at every opportunity. She'd always spend time with me during summer vacations and holidays from school.

I so cherish the day I took Jerry to our family home on Dickerson Street. Carla and her little girlfriend were peeking around the corner of the house all a giggle. I still think I provided my sister with her first puppy love, and she agrees. Carla and Jerry made an instant connection. They adored each other until he left this earth. And so it was when she met her *true* love, Les, her husband to be. Jer was the big brother in our little world. Although Les came from a large family, Jerry was special to him.

Through most of her teen years, Jer and I lived in Michigan not far from my parents and Carla and Les were at our house often in their dating years. It was Carla that came running to help with my older son, Vince, when my youngest son, Bill, was rushed to the emergency room with spinal meningitis. It was Carla who stood by me weeping when we moved away to Ohio a few years and adventures later. But they visited us often it being only a four hour drive away.

Jer and I went home to Michigan so I could be the Matron of Honor at her and Les's wedding. I was so proud of her that day, and so honored that she'd chosen me over her many close friends to stand by her side on her wedding day, the thirteenth of September.

Always, even when distance separated us, we were there for each other or on the phone. When Carla's first daughter was born, I flew to Michigan to feed Amanda her first spoon of cereal. The name Amanda wasn't Amber as I'd dreamed for a first daughter, but close. Carla had the two daughters I never had. Mary followed Amanda. I had the two sons I so adore, a perfect balance, really. Many a wonderful time and gathering took place as our children grew up.

My sister and I were to go through a time of our worst trials, though. We'd been through losing our dear grandmother but were given a chance to prepare, as much as anyone can be for that kind of loss. Gram lived to be almost ninety-one and she was ready to go to her rest those twenty-eight years ago.

The day I called Carla to tell her Jerry had been air-lifted to Atlanta and didn't have much time, there was no hesitation. "We'll be on the next plane," she said.

Carla and Les walked into Jer's room a few hours later. Although, he couldn't speak much as he'd just been taken off the ventilator, he opened his eyes and the old sparkle was there as a grin inched across his face at seeing them. A machine was temporarily pumping his blood through his veins.

Jerry was given the chance to say goodbye as wife, son, sister, and brother in marriage stood by his bed, and we to him, although the word was never uttered. He went in peace the next morning after convincing us to go get a cup of coffee. He didn't want us to see him take the journey we couldn't make with him.

It was the thirteenth of August, the exact same day and date that my grandpa had went on, years before. Friday the thirteenth.

A few days later, my youngest son and I returned to the treehouse in Florida. Bill was still living in Fort Meyers at the time, but Vince, the older, was in Chicago. Carla and Les had returned to Michigan and my parents were up there also after wintering in Florida.

Bill stayed with me for the weekend but had to go back to work on Monday. I was about to experience total and complete solitude for the first time in my life. I didn't handle it well. Lost and devastated, I wanted to go where Jerry had gone.

It was Carla who called me every single day to check on me. On especially hard days, she called twice, morning and evening and talked for as long as it took to calm me. She wanted me to come stay with her but I couldn't leave my house. It was all that was left of what Jer and I had built and shared, and Bill was only an hour away. He would be back on the weekends. She understood and continued to check on me until she was sure I could stand alone. Only Carla. Even my boys gave me credit for more strength than I had, calling only two or three times a week. I wore my brave *mother* facade for them. They'd just lost a dad, after all. Only Carla could see my lost soul.

Jerry's ashes were kept with me a while until I adjusted to the finality. I wanted to take Jer to the headwater in our forest in North Carolina, and I hope to be taken there myself when the time comes. But on that cool mountain day on Easter Sunday, once again it was Carla, Les and their girls that stood beside me and my sons.

Life again went on and circles turned as I've written earlier. But, Carla and I had one more difficult burden to share and bear. The day came when we, again stood side by side at the bed of our dying father. She and I had seen the look that only those about to pass can have. It's in the eyes regardless what words are spoken. Or not.

Dear Papa was able to linger a few more weeks, but he would never come home again. Carla and I knew that down deep, but my mom hadn't accepted it and thought a feeding tube would give him time to recover. My heart ached for I knew what was coming for her. I had to return to Florida to my job, as I was still working to keep the roof over my head. The day the phone rang, even before I heard the voice, I knew Papa had gone on. It was the thirteenth of December, 2005.

Carla was devastated as I'd been several times before. I so ached for her, too. It was Carla that was Papa's *little girl*. He loved us both equally in the end, but he'd been around to bond with her when those bonding things happen. I was more thrust into his arms after a war, and in a time of confusion. I was more Papa's *big girl*. We truly bonded as adults, after both of us had become much wiser. Carla and I were both devastated again for our own reasons.

When Papa died, Carla purchased both of us an identical little stone monument with fiber optic butterflies resting on its stone. The words on the plaque say simply, *"If butterflies could fly to heaven, they would bring my love to you, and yours right back to me."*

We'd already shared the rainbows that Jerry sent and now we shared the butterflies. I look at Papa's little monument every morning as I sit on the breakfast porch with my coffee. This past holiday, a now difficult time for all of us with Papa leaving so close to Christmas, I wrote my sister a poem that, for me says it all . . .

If Butterflies Could Fly to Heaven

If butterflies could fly to heaven
Just what would be their task?
If butterflies could fly to heaven
Would they have many things to ask?

Perhaps, the very question,
Is one, an answer, we'll always lack.
If butterflies could fly to heaven,
Would they even bother to come back?

If butterflies could fly to heaven,
Perhaps, should be asked a different way.
Instead of 'if' butterflies could fly to heaven,
'Why' would be a better word to say.

Butterflies CAN fly to heaven.
Being a messenger is their task.
They transfer wisdom and comfort,
there are no questions which they need ask.

When butterflies fly to heaven,
they unburden, lift us from the black
Speak to who they must,
then bring our answers back.

They carry all our loss and pain
to who we miss, or ask what we need to know.
Then they fly right back to us,
their blessings to bestow.

They travel o'vr the rainbows,
the pathways of the soul,
carrying the love and wisdom
that we desperately need to know.

The next time you see rainbows
arcing across heavenly skies,
watch closely, and perhaps, you'll see,
that the vibrant hues of rainbows,
are the wings of butterflies.

These have been but a few of the thousands of words I've scrawled across a page over my life. My main objective was to leave a few words of posterity for my maternal family. I'm the last one who will write of my grandparents and my father, I suspect. To not share them would be a huge disservice to the next generations of our family. Amanda already has a beautiful daughter named Hannah who won't know these special souls who left before her time here.

My cousin Melanie, my father's sister's daughter has written of the paternal side. Her mom, my Aunt Ginny, played a big role in my life, too. Her children were the *siblings* I had before I had my own sister and I spent a lot of time with Papa's family growing up, as well. My grandmother, Sadie, had eight grandchildren, though, so one more running around wasn't much of a big deal. My dad's father, Isaac, went on before I was born, succumbing to tuberculosis before my dad went to war. My step-grandfather, George, was a kind, hard working man who was good to my grandmother and all us kids. Grandma Sadie and her four children are gone now. Only the widows remain, my mom and dad's brother Jim's wife, Aunt Erma. Erma is in Florida by me. She and Uncle Jim had no children.

Mel and I, both writers, have become very close as adults. She and her husband Jim, whom I also adore, (that's another book) founded and run Proud Spirit Horse Sanctuary, in Mena, Arkansas. It began here in Florida with one horse on five acres. They've now saved and housed nearly two hundred abandoned and abused horses.

I was driven to write this little book for personal reasons and sincerely desire that all my family members and dear friends not mentioned by name, and anyone who happens across these words are somehow touched by the simplicity of the rather ordinary but incredible life that has been mine to live.

Now, I will get back to work on my second novel. It is truly a challenge as it's a work of creative fiction called, *The House is Burning!* Or maybe it isn't fiction at all . . . .

~ Susan C. Haley 2009 ~